[1]

The Ultimate Book

Of

Advanced English Grammar

CONTENTS

1. Parts Of Speech		01
I.	Noun	01
II.	Pronoun	04
III.	Verb	05
IV.	Adjective	07
V.	Adverb	08
VI.	Preposition	10
VII.	Conjunction	12
VIII.	Articles	13
2. Sentence		15
3. Degree Of Comparison		16
4. Gender		18
5. This, That, These, Those		18
6. Tenses		19
I.	Present Tense	19
II.	Past Tense	23
III.	Future Tense	26
1. Present Continuous Tense		29
2. Present Perfect Tense		31
3. Present Perfect Continuous Tense		33
4. Present To be Tense		34
1. Past Continuous Tense		35
2. Past Perfect Tense		37
3. Past Perfect Continuous Tense		38
4. Past To be Tense.		39
1. Future Continuous Tense		40
2. Future Perfect Tense		41
3. Future Perfect Continuous Tense		42
4. Future To be Tense		43

7. Passive Voice/ Active voice — 44

1.	Passive Voice Of Present Tense	44
2.	Passive Voice Of **Past** Tense	46
3.	Passive Voice Of **Future** Tense	48

Passive Voice Of Present Continuous Tense — 49

Passive Voice Of **Present Perfect** Tense — 51

Passive Voice Of Past Continuous Tense — 52

Passive Voice Of **Past Perfect** Tense — 54

Passive Voice Of Future Continuous Tense — 55

Passive Voice Of **Future Perfect** Tense — 57

8. Question Words — 59

What, when, where, who, whom, why, how, which, how come, how old, how much, how many, how long how far.

9. Dubious Tenses — 61

I.	Present Dubious Tense	61
II.	Present Continuous Dubious Tense	63
III.	Present Perfect Dubious Tense	64
IV.	Present Perfect Continuous Dubious Tense	65

Usage of "Must" and "have to" — 66

10. Potential Tenses — 67
I.	Present Potential Tense	67
II.	Past Potential Tense	68
III.	Future Potential Tense	70

Usages of can be and could be — 70

Usages of Couldn't have/Can't have — 71

Usages of Should/Shouldbe/Should have to/Ought to — 71

11. Habitual Tenses		72
I.	Present Habitual Tense	72
II.	Past Habitual Tense	73
Usages of Need/Dare		74
12. Conditional Tenses		75
I.	Real conditionals	75
II.	Unreal conditionals	76
III.	Past conditional tense	76
13. Transitive Verb/ Intransitive Verb		76
14. Gerund/ Infinitive		77
15. Bare infinitive		77

16. Structures		78
I.	Conjunctive Sentences	78
II.	More Usage: was to/were to, was to have/were to have	79
III.	Optative Sentences	79
IV.	Exclamatory Sentences	80
V.	Causative Sentences	80

Not only...but also, Either/or, Either, Neither/nor, Neither, But, Scarcely...when, Hardly/hardly ever, If only, Likely, Seem , It is reported, Unlikely, Like/Unlike, Gonna/Gonna go/Wanna, Cause, More usage of cause, Having said that/However/ On the contrary/On the other hand, Subjunctive sentences, Lest..should, It is time, As though/As if, Even though/Even if, Whether/or, In case, Until, Unless/Until and unless, Since/For, As soon as, As long as, Too, As far as, Way+adjective, Way forward, Way more/ Much more/ Far more, Way too/Much too/ Far too, As much as, Instead, Instead of, About to, Direct/indirect speech, Help, Nevertheless/Nonetheless/Notwithstanding, Having to,Usage of Were, Were to.

PARTS OF SPEECH

1. Noun

2. Pronoun

3. Verb

4. Adjective

5. Adverb

6. Preposition

7. Conjunction

8. Articles

1. NOUN

Noun is a person, place, animal and object.

Basically anything that is a thing is noun.

Noun fall into two categories common noun and proper nouns. Common nouns are general names for things like planet, game show. Proper nouns are specific names for individual things like Jupiter, NASA, and Samsung.

Examples:

Happiness

Cold

Heat

Water

John

Alice

Chair

Table

Truth

Lie

SENTENCES OF NOUN

I didn't have **happiness**.

I want to have **water**.

There is a **table**.

There is a **mobile phone** on the **table**.

She sings a **song**.

Azzan likes to play **cricket**.

Ayesha recites the **Quran**.

Ali is a very intelligent **boy**.

We will send you **invitation** soon.

My **grandfather** was great.

IDENTIFY NOUN

The birds are flying in the sky.

I am driving a car.

President has announced the holidays for Eid eve.

Ayesha will get first position in exams.

She is a student.

He is a teacher.

We have got a success.

I am from Pakistan.

I will buy the clothes.

Her brother is crying.

Noun is a person, place, animal, and object.

Person	Place	Animal	Object/Thing
Ali	Home	Cat	Table
John.	Office.	Lion.	Chair
Alex.	City	Elephant	Flower
Student.	Country	Wale	Mobile phone
Teacher	New York	Shark	Fan
Mom	Larkana	Bee	Air condition
Dad	Kitchen	Pigeon	Pen
Man	Hospital	Deer	Book
Woman	Bank	Goat	Pencil
Boy	University	Cow	Shoe
Grandfather	Zoo	Bear	Apple

2. PRONOUN

A pronoun is a word that takes the place of a noun.

Subjective	Objective	Possessive		Reflexive pronoun
		Adjective Pronoun	Possessive Pronoun	
I	Me	My	Mine	Myself
We	Us	Our	Ours	Ourselves
You	You	Your	Yours	Yourself/Yourselves
He	Him	His	His	Himself
She	Her	Her	Hers	Herself
It	It	Its	Its	Itself
They	Them	Their	Theirs	Theirselves

SENTENCES OF PRONOUN

I miss **my** brother.

Ayesha called **me**.

This mobile phone is **mine**.

We flew to Pakistan last year.

They got a chance.

They are good friends of **ours**.

She will rely on **you**.

I am **yours**.

She beat them **herself**.

I ordered pizza **myself**.

IDENTIFY PRONOUN

I asked from her few questions.

He insisted me to work hard.

I will give him another chance myself.

We are good friends of yours.

You are a friend of ours.

He is our friend.

They are our enemies.

I will answer her.

A car has its own LCD.

It is raining outside.

3. VERB

A verb is a word or combination of the words that indicates an action.

Examples:

Take

Give

Send

Admire

Tell

Walk

Appreciate

Fight

Investigate

Praise

SENTENCES OF VERB

John **walks** in the morning.

Mike is **going** to school.

Albert **likes** to walk.

Anna **is** a good girl.

Azzan **plays** cricket.

Ayesha **recites** the Quran.

He **laughs** at them.

We **are** happy people.

She **asked** from him a question.

IDENTIFY VERB

They are trying to succeed.

She will get her car.

He calls her mom.

Ayesha is a very good student.

He is a good doctor.

They are lying.

You speak the truth.

Azzan is not doing his homework.

Alice strived to get first position in exams.

He praised her beauty.

4. ADJECTIVE

Adjectives are words that describe nouns (or pronouns). "Old," "green," and "cheerful" are examples of adjectives.

Examples:

New

Old

Blue

Happy

Sad

Beautiful

Huge

Big

Small

Intelligent

SENTENCES OF ADJECTIVE

She has a **new** car.

They will buy a **big** house.

I am **happy** today.

He was a **sad** person.

I will give you a **huge** applaud.

Ali is an **intelligent** boy.

She has been a **clever** girl.

We had **many** reasons to quit the party.

He has a **little** doubt.

It creates **abundant** confusion.

IDENTIFY ADJECTIVE

They live in a beautiful house.

Lisa is wearing a sleeveless shirt today.

This soup is not edible.

She wore a beautiful dress.

He writes the meaningful letters.

This shop is even nicer.

She wore a beautiful dress.

Ben is an adorable baby.

Linda's hair is gorgeous.

This glass is breakable.

5. ADVERB

An **adverb** is a word that modifies (describes) a verb (he sings loudly), an adjective (very tall), another **adverb** (ended too quickly), or even a whole sentence (Fortunately, I had brought an umbrella). **Adverbs** often end in -ly, but some (such as fast) look exactly the same as their adjective counterparts.

Position of adverb

Front position: before subject.

Mid position: before main verb.

End position: after object.

Usages

Front position: Luckily I had a chance.

Mid position: I am **hugely** honored.

End position: We will raise money for charity **necessarily**.

EXAMPLES OF ADVERB

Boldly

Bravely

Brightly

Cheerfully

Elegantly

Faithfully

Fortunately

Beautifully

Happily

Honestly

SENTENCES OF ADVERB

I tackled this issue **boldly**.

He fought the fight **bravely**.

Unfortunately, We could not reach on time.

He was **hugely** honored.

I Wrote an article **beautifully**.

She will **extremely** oppose it.

Ayesha prepared for exams **intelligently**.

They talked to her **honestly**.

She **happily** gave him a book.

We reached Larkana **safely**.

IDENTIFY ADVERB

He swims well.

He ran quickly.

She spoke softly.

James coughed loudly to attract her attention.

He plays the flute beautifully.

He ate the chocolate cake greedily.

He greedily ate the chocolate cake.

He gave us the money generously.

He generously gave us the money

6. PREPOSITION

A **preposition** is a word or group of words used before a noun, pronoun, or noun phrase to show direction, time, place, location, spatial relationships, or to introduce an object.

Examples:

in

at

on

of

to

from

above

under

over

SENTECES OF PREPOSITION

There is dust **in** the room.

I will study **at** 5pm.

He will keep mobile phone **on** the desk.

They will talk **to** me.

We will not laugh **at** her.

She will consult **with** doctor.

Alina will go **to** America.

She will live **in** America.

You will work **in** the office.

He sat **on** the chair.

IDENTIFY PREPOSITION

They were sitting by the tree.

We are running in the gym today.

The sun is behind the clouds.

She lives near her workplace.

She drew the picture with a crayon.

He swam at the lake.

I walked down the street.

We located the key for the lock.

The car went through the tunnel.

I got a package from a friend.

7. CONJUNCTION

Conjunctions are words that link other words, phrases, or clauses together.

Examples:

for

and

whenever

but

or

yet

so

Now

Even if

As though

SENTENCES OF CONJUNCTION

I bought my clothes **and** got them stitched.

I will play cricket **but** will not play tennis.

She will select English **or** Mathematics subject.

He brought the books **for** me.

They will call me **even** if they are busy.

He scolded them **as though** he were a minister.

I am working hard **so** I can avail scholarship.

Ali will give medical exams **as soon as** he accomplishes his studies.

Police is patrolling in the streets **whereas** some riots have occurred inside the city.

He is appreciated **because** everyone likes him.

I will play cricket, **likewise** I will play badminton.

IDENTIFY CONJUNCTION

She was tired when she arrived in class, for she had studied all night.

I tried out for the basketball team, but I didn't make it.

It's snowing outside, yet it's the middle of summer!

Monica does not know about Michael and Bobby, nor about Jessica and Susan.

So far, he hasn't told her the truth.

They love football, yet they gave up their tickets to someone less fortunate.

I will strive in my studies, in addition, I will do part time job.

He fought a fight even when he was ill.

She will prove herself as an intellectual.

I see your picture whenever I miss you.

8. Articles

There are three articles: a, an, and the. Articles are used before nouns or noun equivalents and are a type of adjective.

Examples:

a, an, the

SENTENCES OF a, an, the

She plays **the** piano.

Safa is **an** intelligent student.

He plays football.
I have got **a** cold.

She has **a** headache.

I'm **a** teacher.

She goes to **the** prison to see him once **a** month.

I'm going to **the** school to see **the** head master.

She's in hospital at **the** moment.
Her husband goes to **the** hospital to see her every afternoon.

Words which start with Vowels use "an".

Vowels are a e i o u and sometimes y.

Words which start with Consonant use "a".

Plural words often use "the".

Continents, towns and streets don't use articles.

Africa, New York, Crist church St.

Vowels having consonant pronunciation

a vegetable, a university, unity, a vehicle etc.

Consonants having vowel pronunciation.

an hour etc.

IDENTIFY ARTICLES

I brought the vegetables yesterday.

He will give me a book.

She went to the university.

They got an opportunity.

I ate an apple.

She gave him an orange.

We need unity in our lives.

They brought the vehicles for showroom.

It is a good variety of clothes.

He has bought the clothes for a party.

SENTENCE

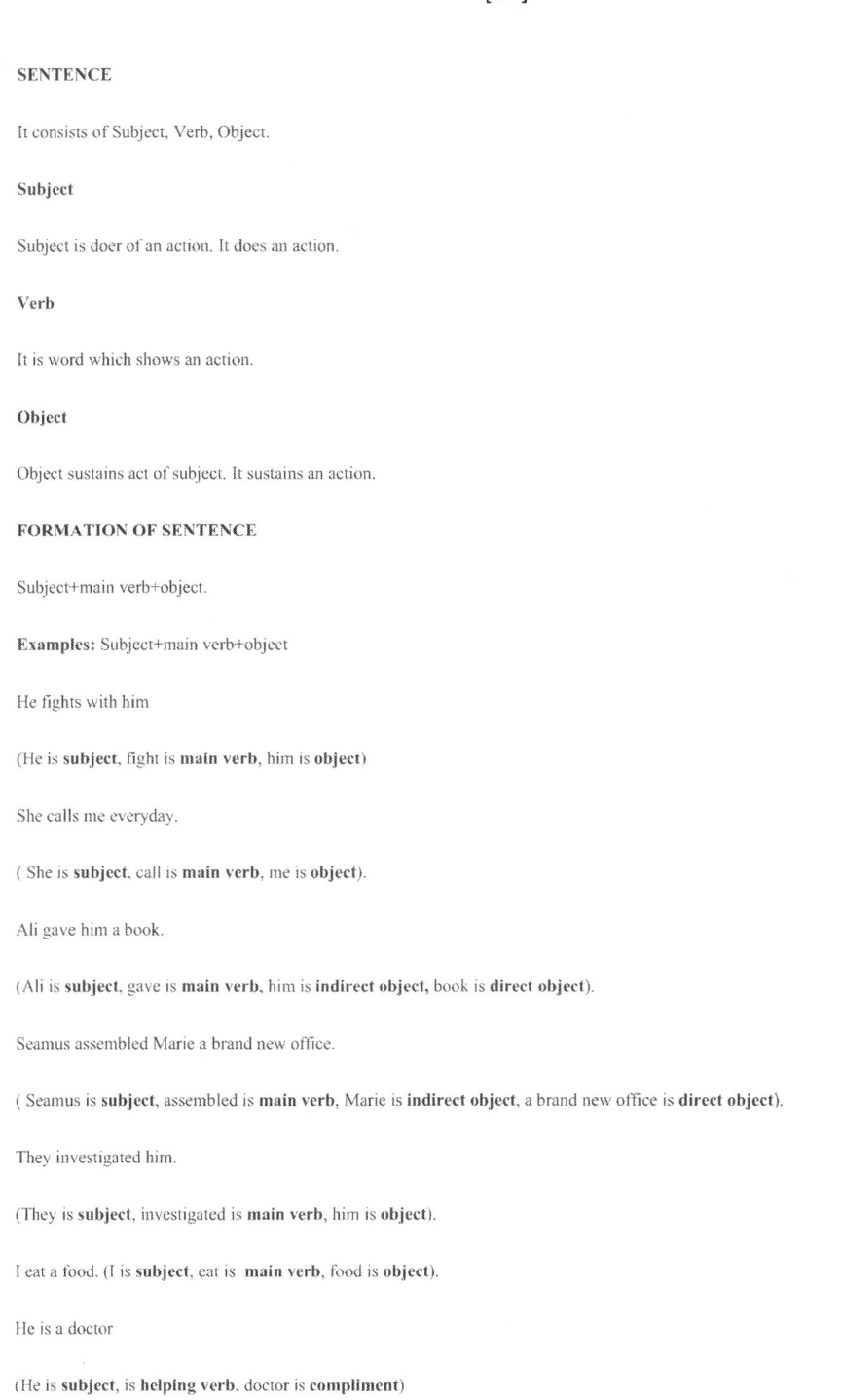

It consists of Subject, Verb, Object.

Subject

Subject is doer of an action. It does an action.

Verb

It is word which shows an action.

Object

Object sustains act of subject. It sustains an action.

FORMATION OF SENTENCE

Subject+main verb+object.

Examples: Subject+main verb+object

He fights with him

(He is **subject**, fight is **main verb**, him is **object**)

She calls me everyday.

(She is **subject**, call is **main verb**, me is **object**).

Ali gave him a book.

(Ali is **subject**, gave is **main verb**, him is **indirect object**, book is **direct object**).

Seamus assembled Marie a brand new office.

(Seamus is **subject**, assembled is **main verb**, Marie is **indirect object**, a brand new office is **direct object**).

They investigated him.

(They is **subject**, investigated is **main verb**, him is **object**).

I eat a food. (I is **subject**, eat is **main verb**, food is **object**).

He is a doctor

(He is **subject**, is **helping verb**, doctor is **compliment**)

She is happy.

(She is **subject**, is **helping verb**, happy is **compliment**) there is no object because there is no action to sustain.

IDENTIFY SUBJECT, VERB, OBJECT.

Sasha paints landscapes.

I ate an apple.

They had dinner at restaurant last night.

We are happy.

He is a doctor.

Azzan plays cricket at home.

She appreciated them.

You got a good chance.

He studied English literature at Harvard University.

They fought a war against their enemies.

DEGREE OF COMPARISON

Positive degree

Comparative degree

Superlative degree

Positive degree

The positive degree merely speaks of a quality of thing or people. It is used with no comparison.

A car is cheap.

He is smart.

Comparative degree

The comparison degree is used when two things and people are compared.

A car is cheaper.

John is smarter than Mike.

Superlative degree

The superlative degree is used to compare one member of a group with the whole group.

He is the greatest in the world.

She is the tallest in sisters.

Positive	Comparative	Superlative
Late.	Later.	Latest
Smart.	Smarter.	Smartest
Wise.	Wiser.	Wisest
Fine.	Finer.	Finest

GENDER

Masculine Gender

Boy, man, father, husband.

Feminine Gender

Girl, bride, mother, wife.

Neuter Gender

Blackboard, chalk, chair, orange.

Common Gender

Friend, teacher, leader, cousin.

This, That, These, Those.

This, that, these and those are demonstratives. We use this, that, these and those to point to people and things. This and that are singular. These and those are plural. We use them as determiners and pronouns.

Determiners

1. What's in this box?

2. That water tastes strange.

3. I might get myself a pair of those shoes.

Pronoun

1. Come and look at this.

2. That's a very good idea.

3. Can I have one of these?

TENSES

1. PRESENT TENSE

2. PAST TENSE

3. FUTURE TENSE

PRESENT TENSE

The present tense is used to talk about the present and to talk about the future.

Sentence: Subject+verb+Object

They fight with him.   **(Present tense.)**

It has two meanings.

1. They simply fight with him at a moment.

2. They always fight with him.

He calls me   **(Present tense).**

It has two meanings.

1. He simply calls me at a moment

2. He always calls me.

In addition, he is third person singular that's why we put "s" or "es" with verb. Here verb is call and after putting "s" with verb it becomes calls.

Pronoun

Subjective pronoun

First person

I   **Singular**

We   **Plural**

Second person

You   **Singular**

You   **Plural**

Third person

He	**Singular**
She	**Singular**
It	**Singular**
They	**Plural**

Singular.   Only one.

Plural.   More than one.

Plural noun words

To make plural we put "s" or "es" with noun.

Orange= Oranges

Book= books

Mango= mangoes/mangos

Class= classes

Fox= foxes

Examples for Present tense.

He speaks the truth.

She tells a lie.

They motivate him.

I like to write the articles.

We ask you about your marriage.

Azzan plays cricket.

Ayesha recites the Quran.

He goes shopping.

She goes swimming.

Safa wants to be an accountant.

There are three types of sentence in every tense.

Affirmative sentence   He eats a food.

Negative sentence   He does not eat a food.

Interrogative sentence   Does he eat a food?

We have already learnt about affirmative sentences.

We use helping verbs/ auxiliary verbs "**do**" and "**does**" to make negative or interrogative sentences. We use "**do**" with plural subject and "**you**". Whereas we use "**does**" with third person singular subject in order to make either negative or interrogative sentences. We don't put "s" with verb using third person singular subject while making negative or interrogative sentences through does or does not.

NEGATIVE SENTENCE

We show that an action is not occurring in this type of sentence. We use "**do**" or "**does**" along with "**not**" to make negative sentence

Do not, does not

In contraction We use don't for do not and doesn't for does not.

He doesn't irritate them.

She doesn't call you.

Azzan doesn't fight with Ayesha.

I don't blame you.

They don't want a new car.

INTERROGATIVE SENTENCE

We ask a question in interrogative sentence. We use do or does before subject and put question mark at the end of sentence in order to make interrogative sentence.

Do you want to go abroad?

Does she rely on you?

Do we get response from him?

Do they fight with her?

Does he cook a food?

NEGATIVE AND INTERROGATIVE SENTENCE

Do you not want to go abroad?

Does she not rely on you?

Contraction

Don't you want to go abroad?

Doesn't she rely on you?

Use of **has** and **have** in present and **had** in past tenses. Its primary meaning is "to possess, own, hold for use, or contain." **Have** and **has** and **had** indicate possession in the present and past tenses.

He has a pen.

They have English teacher.

We don't have a certainty.

You had a car.

She does not have a mobile phone.

Has and have in question.

Have you been to America.

Who has my phone?

Has/have got and Has/have (same thing)

I have got a book. (I have a book)

She has got a car. (She has a car)

Has to and have to

He has to work hard.

We have to finish our home work today.

She doesn't have to get there.

I have to call her.

PAST TENSE

The past tense is the verb tense used for a past activity or a past state of being.

Example. Subject+verb+object

He ate a food.

They gave him a book.

We use second form of main verb (Past) in past tense.

In first sentence, he ate a food in past. Or in time which is gone.

Likewise in second sentence, they gave him a book in past. Or in time which is gone.

NEGATIVE SENTENCE

We show that an action is not occurring in this type of sentence. We use "**did not**" or "**didn't**" to make negative sentence in past tense.

He didn't irritate them.

She did not call you.

Azzan did not fight with Ayesha.

I didn't blame you.

They didn't want a new car.

INTERROGATIVE SENTENCE

We ask a question in interrogative sentence. We use did before subject and put question mark at the end of sentence in order to make interrogative sentence in past tense.

Did you want to go abroad?

Did she rely on you?

Did we get response from him?

Did they fight with her?

Did he cook a food?

Did Azzan study daily?

NEGATIVE AND INTERROGATIVE SENTENCE

Did you not want to go abroad?

Did she not rely on you?

Contraction

Didn't you want to go abroad?

Didn't she reply on you?

Few examples of verbs(words).

Present	Past	Past Participle	Present Participle
First form of verb	**Second form of verb**	**Third form of verb**	**Fourth form of verb**
Eat	ate	eaten	eating
Give	gave	given	giving
Call	called	called	calling
Fight	fought	fought	fighting
Send	sent	sent	sending
Cut	cut	cut	cutting
Blame	blamed	blamed	blaming
Do	did	done	doing

Examples for Past tense

[25]

He brought mobile phone from Dubai.

We went to Dubai last year

They apologized from me.

He sent her a message.

She bought a laptop.

Azzan went swimming in a pool.

Ayesha did her homework.

He invited her on dinner.

Ayesha strived to get 1st position in her exams.

They ignored her.

FUTURE TENSE

The future tense is the verb tense used to describe a future event or state of being.

Example:

Subject+Will/Shall/would (helping verb)+main verb+object.

He will read your letter tomorrow.

I shall buy a new car.

Would: we use **would** with all pronouns (subject) instead of will or shall.

Shall : we tradionally use **Shall** with first form pronoun(subject).

Will: we traditionally use **Will** with Second and third form pronoun(subject).

Usually we can use **will** with all first, second, and third form pronouns (subject).

In first sentence, he **will** read newspaper tomorrow in future. It means there is still time when he will read newspaper in future.

Likewise in second sentence, I will buy a new car in coming time like in future.

Contraction

I'll for I will/I shall

He'll for he will

To emphasize we use **shall** with second and third form pronouns(subject) instead of **will** in the sentence.

He shall try to win a competition.

In above sentence, there is emphasis that he will certainly try to win a competition.

NEGATIVE SENTENCE

We show that an action is not occurring in this type of sentence. We use "**will not**" or "**shall not**" to make negative sentence in future tense.

Contraction

Won't for will not

Shan't for shall not

He won't irritate them.

She will not call you.

Azzan will not fight with Ayesha.

I won't blame you.

They won't want a new car.

INTERROGATIVE SENTENCE

We ask a question in interrogative sentence. We use will or shall before subject and put question mark at the end of sentence in order to make interrogative sentence in future tense.

Will you want to go abroad?

Will she rely on you?

Will we get response from him?

Will they fight with her?

Will he cook a food?

Will Azzan study daily?

NEGATIVE AND INTERROGATIVE SENTENCE

Will you not want to go abroad?

Will she not rely on you?

Contraction

Won't you want to go abroad?

Won't she rely on you?

Examples for future tense

Azzan will take an interest in studies one day.

They will run a new business.

He will give us another chance.

We will take his interview.

She will purchase new gadget soon.

Ayesha will call them.

Pakistan will succeed in developing its economy one day.

People will take corona precautions.

False will always take you to the wrong direction.

It will make difference.

There are four more types of every tenses.

1. PRESENT CONTINOUS TENSE

2. PRESENT PERFECT TENSE

3. PRESENT PERFECT CONTINOUS TENSE

4. PRESENT TO BE TENSE

1. PAST CONTINOUS TENSE

2. PAST PERFECT TENSE

3. PAST PERFECT CONTINOUS TENSE

4. PAST TO BE TENSE

1. FUTURE CONTINUOUS TENSE

2. FUTURE PERFECT TENSE

3. FUTURE PERFECT CONTINOUS TENSE

4. FUTURE TO BE TENSE

PRESENT CONTINOUS TENSE

The present continuous tense is used for actions happening now or for an action that is unfinished as continous action.

Example: Subject+helping verb(to be verb)+ present participle verb(verb-ing)+object.

To be verb(helping verb/auxiliary verb)

Is, am, are

is: we use **is** with third person singular pronoun(subject).

am : we use **am** with I.

are: we use **are** with first person plural, second person singular and plural, and third person plural pronouns(subject).

They are going to Karachi.

Azzan is playing cricket.

He is calling Jennifer.

She is having dinner.

We are speaking the truth.

In above sentences, an action is continuing in present time.

Contraction:

I'm for I am

We're for we are

You're for you are

He's for he is

She's for she is

It's or its for it is

They're for they are

NEGATIVE SENTENCES

Contraction

ain't for am not, is not, are not, has not, have not.

isn't for is not

aren't for are not

He isn't irritating them.

She is not calling you.

Azzan isn't fighting with Ayesha.

I am not blaming you.

They are not wanting a new car.

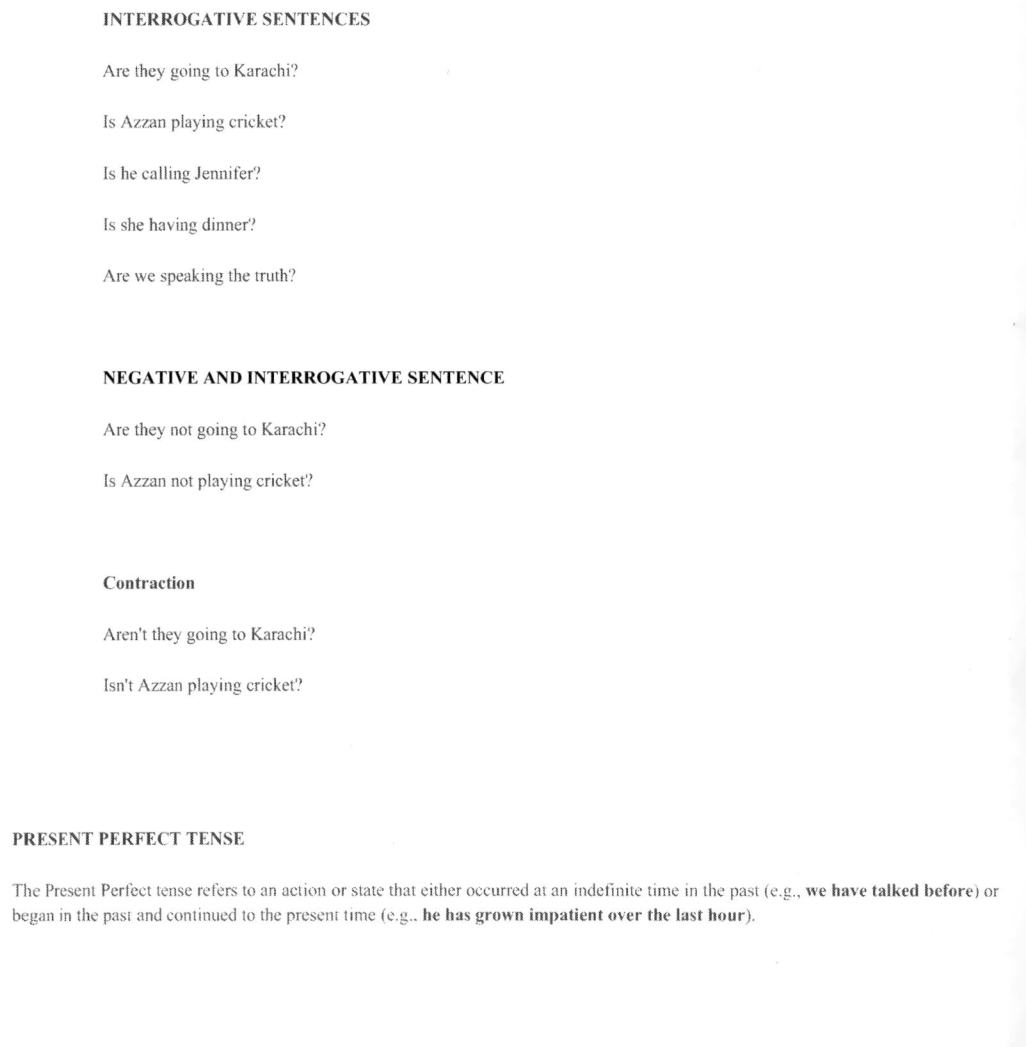

INTERROGATIVE SENTENCES

Are they going to Karachi?

Is Azzan playing cricket?

Is he calling Jennifer?

Is she having dinner?

Are we speaking the truth?

NEGATIVE AND INTERROGATIVE SENTENCE

Are they not going to Karachi?

Is Azzan not playing cricket?

Contraction

Aren't they going to Karachi?

Isn't Azzan playing cricket?

PRESENT PERFECT TENSE

The Present Perfect tense refers to an action or state that either occurred at an indefinite time in the past (e.g., **we have talked before**) or began in the past and continued to the present time (e.g., **he has grown impatient over the last hour**).

Example:

Subject+helping verb+past participle verb+object.

Helping verbs

Has: we use **has** with third person singular pronoun(subject)

Have: we use **have** with first person, second person and third person plural pronouns(subject).

Sentences of present perfect tense

They have gone to Karachi.

Azzan has played cricket.

He has called Jennifer.

She has had dinner.

We have spoken the truth.

Contraction

I've for I have

We've for we have

You've for you have

He's for he has

She's for she has

It's for it has

They've for they have

NEGATIVE SENTENCES

Contraction

hasn't for has not

haven't for have not

They haven't gone to Karachi.

Azzan has not played cricket.

INTERROGATIVE SENTENCES

Have they gone to Karachi?

Has Azzan played cricket?

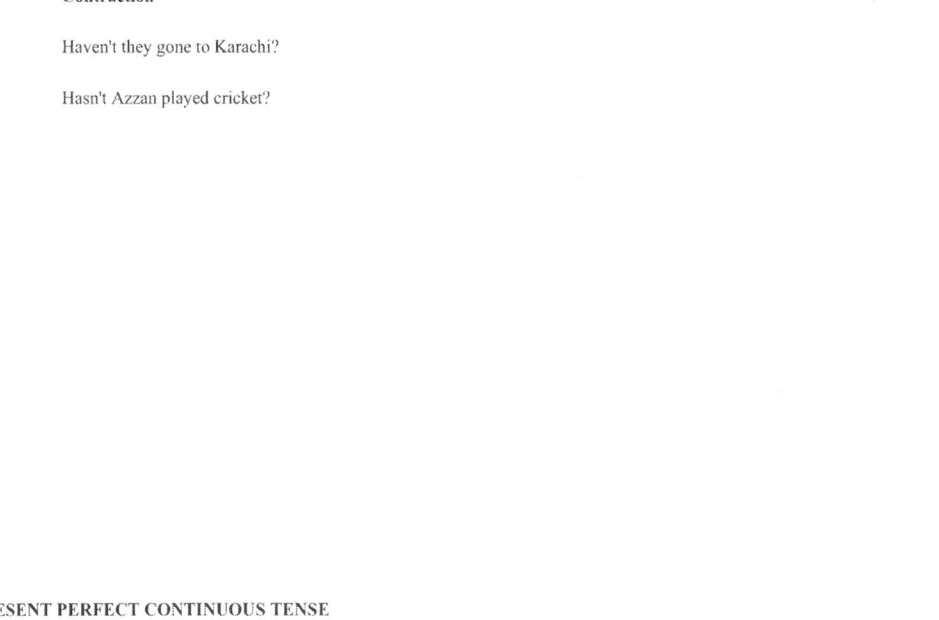

NEGATIVE AND INTERROGATIVE SENTENCE

Have they not gone to Karachi?

Has Azzan not played cricket?

Contraction

Haven't they gone to Karachi?

Hasn't Azzan played cricket?

PRESENT PERFECT CONTINUOUS TENSE

Present Perfect Continuous tense represents the work which started in the **past** and is still running. It uses "**have been/has been**" and "ing" is added with the **verb**.

Example:

Subject+helping verb(has been/have been)+present participle verb(ing-verb)+object.

They have been accusing Govt.

Azzan has been playing cricket for an hour.

He's been calling Jennifer.

They've been having dinner at restaurant for few years.

We have been speaking the truth.

NEGATIVE SENTENCES

They have not been accusing Govt.

Azzan hasn't been playing cricket for an hour.

INTERROGATIVE SENTENCES

Have they been accusing Govt.?

Has Azzan been playing cricket for an hour?

NEGATIVE AND INTERROGATIVE SENTENCE

Have they not been accusing Govt.?

Has Azzan not been playing cricket for an hour?

Contraction

Haven't they been accusing Govt.?

Hasn't Azzan been playing cricket for an hour?

PRESENT TO BE TENSE

Present To Be" is used to show a state of existence in Present.

Example:

Subject+to be verb(is/am/are)+complement.

We are happy.

He is a good doctor.

She's sure.

They are late.

You're sad.

NEGATIVE SENTENCES

We aren't happy.

He is not a good doctor.

INTERROGATIVE SENTENCES

Are we happy?

Is he a good doctor?

NEGATIVE AND INTERROGATIVE SENTENCE

Aren't we happy?

Is he not a good doctor?

PAST CONTINUOUS TENSE

Past Continuous tense is used when the action was ongoing till a certain time in the past. This tense is used to talk about an action at a particular time in the past.

Example:

Subject+was/were(helping verbs)+present participle verb+object.

Was: we use **was** with first person singular and third person singular pronoun(subject).

Were: we use **were** with first person plural, second person singular or plural and third person plural pronoun(subject).

I was writing an article.

We were having dinner last night.

My friends were calling me.

He was going to Karachi.

Azzan was playing cricket.

Contraction

There is no natural contraction for I was.

We're for we were

You're for you were

He's for he was

She's for she was

It's for it was

They're for they were

NEGATIVE SENTENCES

I was not writing an article.

We weren't having dinner last night.

Contraction

Wasn't for was not.

Weren't for were not.

INTERROGATIVE SENTENCES

Was I writing an article?

Were they going to Karachi?

NEGATIVE AND INTERROGATIVE SENTENCE

Wasn't I writing an article?

Were they not going to Karachi?

PAST PERFECT TENSE

The past perfect tense describes a completed activity in the past. It is used to emphasize that an action was completed before another action took place.

Example:

Subject+had(helping verb)+past participle verb(third form of verb)+object.

They had painted the fence before I had a chance to speak to them.

He had bought the clothes last year.

She had called me.

They had accused Govt.

Azzan had taken part in school competition few years ago.

In above sentences, an action completed long time ago in past.

NEGATIVE SENTENCES

They had not painted the fence before I had a chance to speak to them.

He hadn't bought the clothes last year.

INTERROGATIVE SENTENCES

Had they painted the fence before I had a chance to speak to them?

Had he bought the clothes last year?

NEGATIVE AND INTERROGATIVE SENTENCE

Hadn't they painted the fence before I had a chance to speak to them?

Had he not bought the clothes last year?

PAST PERFECT CONTINUOUS TENSE

Past Perfect continuous tense shows that an action that started in the past continued up until another time in the past.

Example:

Subject+had been(helping verb)+present participle verb+object.

He had been calling her.

She had been complaining against police.

They had been slandering one of their friends.

Azzan had been taking part in the school competition.

We had been making money in the business.

NEGATIVE SENTENCES

He hadn't been calling her.

She had not been complaining against police.

INTERROGATIVE SENTENCES

Had he been calling her?

Had she been complaining against police?

NEGATIVE AND INTERROGATIVE SENTENCE

Hadn't he been calling her?

Had she not been complaining against police?

PAST TO BE TENSE

Past To Be" is used to show a state of existence in past.

Example

Subject+was/were(helping verb)+complement.

We were happy.

Bus was so crowded.

She was sure.

Movie was exciting.

They were very angry.

NEGATIVE SENTENCES

We were not happy.

Movie wasn't exciting.

INTERROGATIVE SENTENCES

Were we happy?

Was movie exciting?

NEGATIVE AND INTERROGATIVE SENTENCE

Were we not happy?

Wasn't movie exciting?

FUTURE CONTINUOUS TENSE

Future Continuous tense shows a continuous action which will occur in the future.

Example:

Subject+Will be/shall be(helping verb)+present participle verb+object.

He'll be calling her.

She will be complaining against police.

They will be slandering one of their friends.

Jennifer will be taking part in the school competition.

We'll be making money in the business.

NEGATIVE SENTENCES

Contraction

Won't be for will not be

Shan't be for shall not be

He won't be calling her.

She will not be complaining against police.

INTERROGATIVE SENTENCES

Will he be calling her?

Will she be complaining against police?

NEGATIVE AND INTERROGATIVE SENTENCE

Won't he be calling her?

Will she not be complaining against police?

FUTURE PERFECT TENSE

Future Perfect Tense is used to express an action which, the speaker assumes, will have completed or occurred in the future. It gives a sense of completion of task that will occur in the future.

Example:

Subject+Will have/shall have(helping verb)+past participle verb+object.

He'll have called her.

She will have complained against police.

They will have slandered one of their friends.

Jennifer will have taken part in the school competition.

We'll have made money in the business.

NEGATIVE SENTENCES

he won't have called her.

She will not have complained against police.

INTERROGATIVE SENTENCES

Will he have called her?

Will she have complained against police?

NEGATIVE AND INTERROGATIVE SENTENCE

Will he not have called her?

Won't she have complained against police?

FUTURE PERFECT CONTINOUS TENSE

Future Perfect Continuous Tense shows a continuous action which will be done at a certain time in the future. If two actions take place in the future, the first one which will be continued is **Future Perfect Continuous Tense** and the second one is **Simple Present Tense.**

Example:

Subject+Will have been/shall have been(helping verb)+present participle verb+object.

She will have been complaining against police.

Jennifer will have been taking part in the school competition.

We'll have been making money in the business.

They will have been playing football in that field before you reach.

I will have been attending the program before I come here.

NEGATIVE SENTENCES

She won't have been complaining against police.

Jennifer will not have been taking part in the school competition.

INTERROGATIVE SENTENCES

Will she have been complaining against police?

Will Jennifer have been taking part in the school competition?

NEGATIVE AND INTERROGATIVE SENTENCE

Won't she have been complaining against police?

Won't Jennifer have been taking part in the school competition?

FUTURE TO BE TENSE

Future To Be" is used to show a state of existence in future.

Example:

Subject+Will be/shall be+complement.

We'll be happy.

Bus will be so crowded.

She will be sure.

Movie will be exciting.

They'll be very angry.

NEGATIVE SENTENCES

We won't be happy.

Movie won't be exciting.

INTERROGATIVE SENTENCES

Will we be happy?

Will movie be exciting?

NEGATIVE AND INTERROGATIVE SENTENCE

Won't we be happy?

Won't movie be exciting?

ACTIVE VOICE AND PASSIVE VOICE

ACTIVE VOICE

When the subject of a sentence performs the verb's action, we say that the sentence is in the active voice.

PASSIVE VOICE

Passive voice means that a subject is a recipient of a verb's action.

Example:

He writes an email.   **Present Tense/Active voice**

An email is written by him.   **Passive voice**

Passive voice

Object+helping verb of tense+past participle verb+by+subject.

In above sentence, an action of writing an email is done by him. **He** is converted into object **him** thus all pronouns(subject) are converted into their pronouns(object) to make passive voice sentences. Subject is actually object and object is actually subject. We use **by** before object(subject).

Active voice

I call them.

Azzan plays cricket.

Passive voice

They are called by me

Cricket is played by Azzan.

PASSIVE VOICE OF PRESENT TENSE

Helping verbs

is, am, are

Example: Passive voice

Subject(object)+is/am/are+past participle verb+by+object(subject).

Active voice

He calls me.

They blame police.

Passive voice

I am called by him.

Police is blamed by them.

Another method: We use **get** instead of is,am,are.

Example:

Subject(object)+get+past participle verb+by+object(subject).

Active voice

He calls me.

They blame police.

Passive voice

I get called by him.

Police gets blamed by them.

NEGATIVE SENTENCES

He doesn't call them.

They don't blame police.

PASSIVE VOICE

They aren't called by him.

Police isn't blamed by them.

INTERROGATIVE SENTENCES

Does he call them?

Do they blame police?

Are they called by him?

Is police blamed by them?

NEGATIVE AND INTERROGATIVE SENTENCE

Doesn't he call them?

Don't they blame police?

Aren't they called by him?

Isn't police blamed by them?

PASSIVE VOICE OF PAST TENSE

Helping verbs

was, were

Example: Passive voice

Subject(object)+was/were+past participle verb+by+object(subject).

Active voice

He called me.

They blamed police.

Passive voice

I was called by him.

Police was blamed by them.

Another method: We use **got** instead of was, were.

Example:

Subject(object)+got+past participle verb+by+object(subject).

Active voice

He called me.

They blamed police.

Passive voice

I got called by him.

Police got blamed by them.

NEGATIVE SENTENCES

He didn't call them.

They didn't blame police.

PASSIVE VOICE

They were not called by him.

Police wasn't blamed by them.

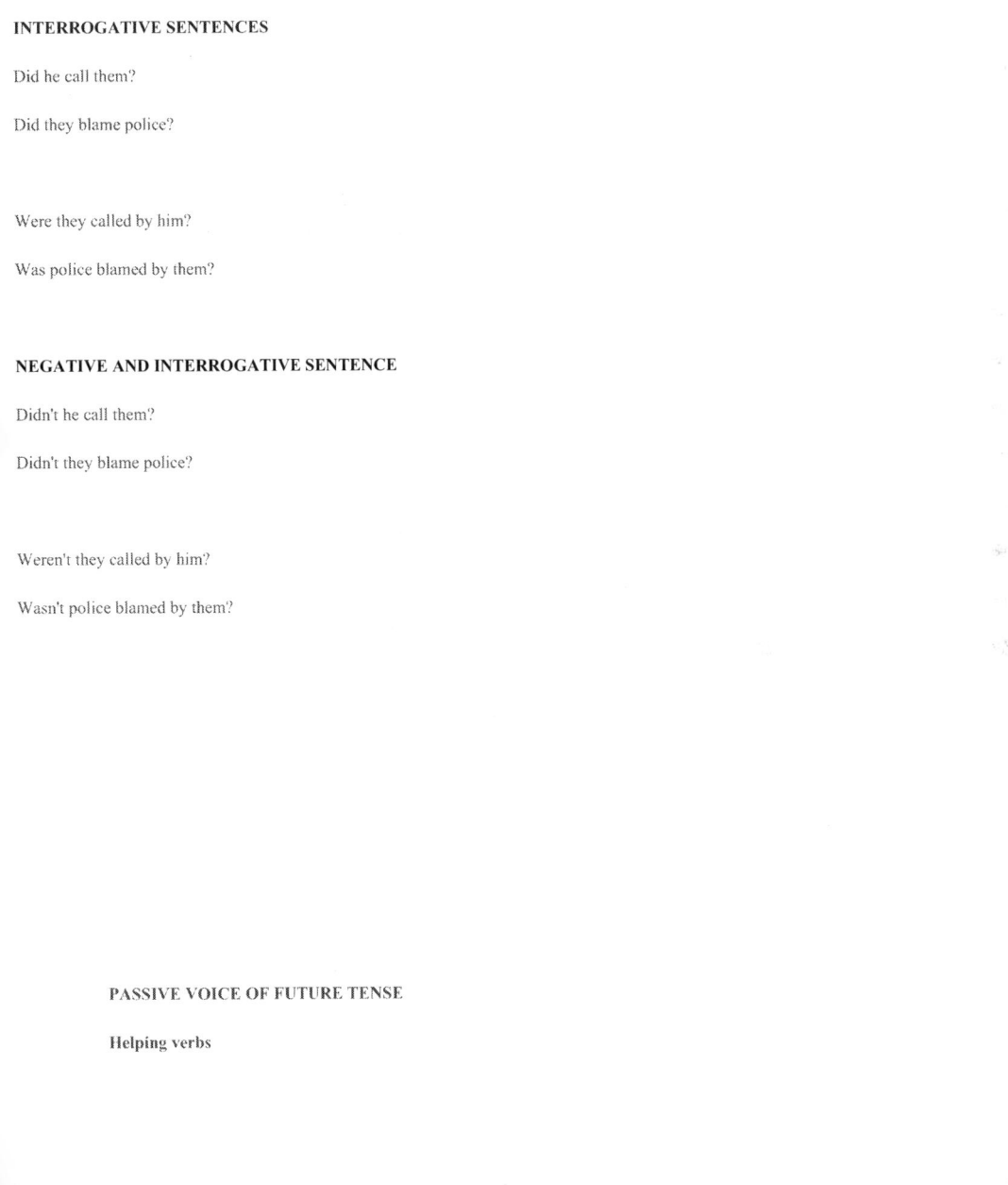

INTERROGATIVE SENTENCES

Did he call them?

Did they blame police?

Were they called by him?

Was police blamed by them?

NEGATIVE AND INTERROGATIVE SENTENCE

Didn't he call them?

Didn't they blame police?

Weren't they called by him?

Wasn't police blamed by them?

PASSIVE VOICE OF FUTURE TENSE

Helping verbs

Will be, shall be

Example: Passive voice

Subject(object)+will be/shall be+past participle verb+by+object(subject).

Active voice

He'll call me.

They will blame police.

Passive voice

I will be called by him.

Police will be blamed by them.

Another method: We use **will/shall get** instead of will, shall.

Example:

Subject(object)+will get/shall get+past participle verb+by+object(subject).

Active voice

He'll call me.

They'll blame police.

Passive voice

I'll get called by him.

Police will get blamed by them.

NEGATIVE SENTENCES

He won't call them.

They won't blame police.

PASSIVE VOICE

They won't be called by him.

Police won't be blamed by them.

INTERROGATIVE SENTENCES

Will he call them?

Will they blame police?

Will they be called by him?

Will police be blamed by them?

NEGATIVE AND INTERROGATIVE SENTENCE

Won't he call them?

Won't they blame police?

Won't they be called by him?

Won't police be blamed by them?

PASSIVE VOICE OF PRESENT CONTINUOUS TENSE

Example:

Subject+is,am,are+being+ past participle verb+by+object.

Helping verbs

is, am, are +being

Active voice

He is calling them.

They are blaming police.

Passive voice

They're being called by him.

Police is being blamed by them.

> **Another method:** We use Present participle verb of **get**.
>
> **Example:**

Subject(object)+is,am,are+getting+past participle verb+by+object(subject).

Active voice

He's calling them.

They're blaming police.

Passive voice

They're getting called by him.

Police is getting blamed by them.

NEGATIVE SENTENCES

He isn't calling them.

They are not blaming police.

PASSIVE VOICE

They aren't being called by him.

Police isn't being blamed by them.

INTERROGATIVE SENTENCES

Is he calling them?

Are they blaming police?

Are they being called by him?

Is police being blamed by them?

NEGATIVE AND INTERROGATIVE SENTENCE

Isn't he calling them?

Aren't they blaming police?

Aren't they being called by him?

Isn't police being blamed by them?

PASSIVE VOICE OF PRESENT PERFECT TENSE

Helping verbs

has been, have been

Example: Passive voice

Subject(object)+has been/have been+past participle verb+by+object(subject).

Active voice

He's called them

They've blamed police.

Passive voice

They've been called by him.

Police has been blamed by them.

Another method:

Example:

Subject(object)+has got/have got+past participle verb+by+object(subject).

Active voice

He's called them.

They've blamed police.

Passive voice

They've got called by him.

Police has got blamed by them.

NEGATIVE SENTENCES

He hasn't called them.

They haven't blamed police.

PASSIVE VOICE

    They haven't been called by him.

    Police hasn't been blamed by them.

INTERROGATIVE SENTENCES

Has he called them?

Have they blamed police?

Have they been called by him?

Has police been blamed by them?

NEGATIVE AND INTERROGATIVE SENTENCE

Hasn't he called them?

Haven't they blamed police?

Haven't they been called by him?

Hasn't police been blamed by them?

PASSIVE VOICE OF PAST CONTINUOUS TENSE

Helping verbs

was, were + being

Example: Passive voice

Subject(object)+was/were+being+past participle verb+by+object(subject).

Active voice

He was calling them.

They were blaming police.

Passive voice

They were being called by him.

Police was being blamed by them.

Another method:

Example:

Subject(object)+were/was+getting+past participle verb+by+object(subject).

Active voice

He was calling them.

They were blaming police.

Passive voice

They were getting called by him.

Police was getting blamed by them.

NEGATIVE SENTENCES

He wasn't calling them.

They were not blaming police.

PASSIVE VOICE

They weren't being called by him.

Police wasn't being blamed by them.

INTERROGATIVE SENTENCES

Was he calling them?

Were they blaming police?

Were they being called by him?

Was police being blamed by them?

NEGATIVE AND INTERROGATIVE SENTENCE

Wasn't he calling them?

Weren't they blaming police?

Weren't they being called by him?

Wasn't police being blamed by them?

PASSIVE VOICE OF PAST PERFECT TENSE

Helping verbs

had been

Example: Passive voice

Subject(object)+had been+past participle verb+by+object(subject).

Active voice

He'd called them

They had blamed police.

Passive voice

They had been called by him.

Police had been blamed by them.

Another method:

Example:

Subject(object)+had got+past participle verb+by+object(subject).

Active voice

He'd called them.

They had blamed police.

Passive voice

They had got called by him.

Police had got blamed by them.

NEGATIVE SENTENCES

He hadn't called them.

They hadn't blamed police.

PASSIVE VOICE

They hadn't been called by him.

Police had not been blamed by them.

INTERROGATIVE SENTENCES

Had he called them?

Had they blamed police?

Had they been called by him?

Had police been blamed by them?

NEGATIVE AND INTERROGATIVE SENTENCE

Had he not called them?

Hadn't they blamed police?

Had they not been called by him?

Hadn't police been blamed by them?

PASSIVE VOICE OF FUTURE CONTINOUS TENSE

Helping verbs

Will be/shall be + being

Example: Passive voice

Subject(object)+will be/shall be+being+past participle verb+by+object(subject).

Active voice

He will be calling them.

They will be blaming police.

    Passive voice

    They will be being called by him.

Police will be being blamed by them.

Another method:

Example:

Subject(object)+will be/shall be+getting+past participle verb+by+object(subject).

Active voice

He will be calling them.

They'll be blaming police.

Passive voice

They will be getting called by him.

Police will be getting blamed by them.

NEGATIVE SENTENCES

He will not be calling them.

They will not be blaming police.

PASSIVE VOICE

They will not be being called by him.

Police will not be being blamed by them.

INTERROGATIVE SENTENCES

Will he be calling them?

Will they be blaming police?

Will they be being called by him?

Will police be being blamed by them?

NEGATIVE AND INTERROGATIVE SENTENCE

Won't he be calling them?

Will they not be blaming police?

Won't they be being called by him?

Will police not be being blamed by them?

PASSIVE VOICE OF FUTURE PERFECT TENSE

Helping verbs

Will have, shall have +been

Example: Passive voice

Subject(object)+will have been/shall have been+past participle verb+by+object(subject).

Active voice

He'll have called them.

They will have blamed police.

Passive voice

They will have been called by him.

Police will have been blamed by them.

Another method:

Example:

Subject(object)+will have/shall have+got+past participle verb+by+object(subject).

Active voice

He'll have called them.

They'll have blamed police.

Passive voice

They will have got called by him.

Police will have got blamed by them.

NEGATIVE SENTENCES

He won't have called them.

They won't have blamed police.

PASSIVE VOICE

They won't have been called by him.

Police won't have been blamed by them.

INTERROGATIVE SENTENCES

Will he have called them?

Will they have blamed police?

Will they have been called by him?

Will police have been blamed by them?

NEGATIVE AND INTERROGATIVE SENTENCE

Won't he have called them?

Won't they have blamed police?

Won't they have been called by him?

Won't police have been blamed by them?

QUESTION WORDS

What, when, where, who, whom, why, how, which, how come, how old, how much, how many, how long how far.

We use these question words to ask a question in all tenses. We use one of these words in starting and put question mark at the end of sentence. We sometimes use preposition with these words. Sometimes we don't use helping verbs before subject.

Example:

What : asking for information about something.

What does he look like?

What do you want in dinner?

Or

What you want in dinner?

To what extent you can take risk.

When : asking about time.

When will you come home?

When did he complete his studies?

Where : asking in or at what place or position.

Where do you live?

Where would you prefer to go?

Sometimes when we don't use helping verb before subject, we don't use question mark in sentence. These sentences mean word by word instead of a question.

When you came home.

Where you live.

When you hurt him.

Who: asking what or which person or people (subject).

whom: asking what or which person or people (object).

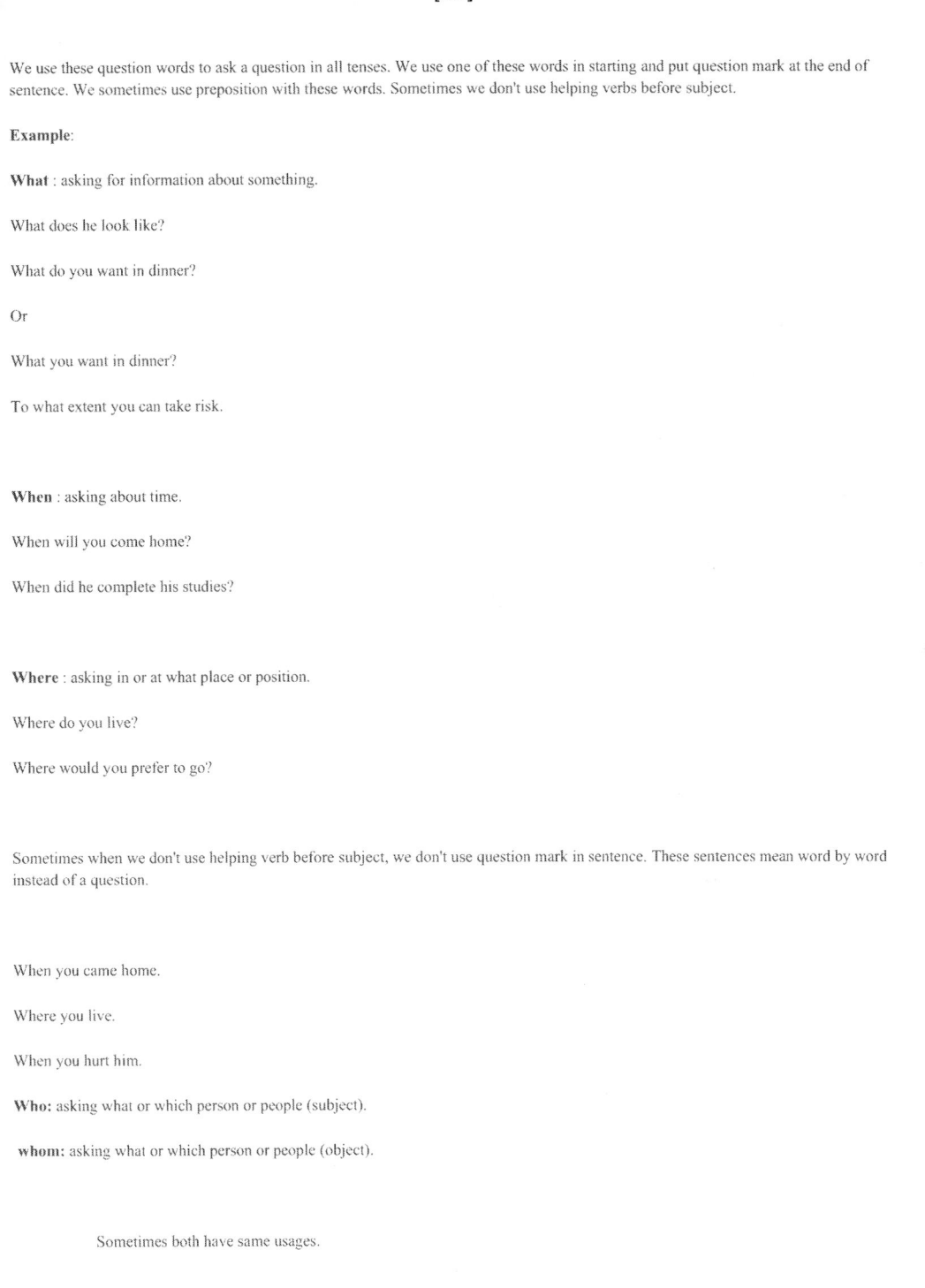

Sometimes both have same usages.

Who are you?

Who do you want to talk to?

Or

Whom do you want to talk to?

Or

To who do you want to talk?

Or

To whom do you want to talk?

Why: asking for reason.

Why did you go there?

Or

How come you went there?

We don't use helping verb before subject while using **how come** in the sentence. **How come** means **how** or **why**?

How come you fight with them?

It means..

Why do you fight with them?

How: asking about manner.

How was your trip?

Which: asking about choice.

Which/what is your favorite fruit?

Which friend likes you the most?

How far: distance

How far New York is from Washington dc?

How long: length (time or space).

How long will it take?

How many: quantity (countable).

How many of you passed the test?

How much: quantity(uncountable).

How much money do you have?

How old: age

How old are you?

DUBIOUS TENSES

PRESENT DUBIOUS TENSE

PRESENT CONTINUOUS DUBIOUS TENSE

PRESENT PERFECT DUBIOUS TENSE

PRESENT PERFECT CONTINUOUS DUBIOUS TENSE

PRESENT DUBIOUS TENSE

A verb showing a dubitative condition of some action in present time is called present dubious tense.

Helping verbs:

may, might

Example:

Subject+may/might+1st form of verb(Present)+object.

We use may or might meaning same thing in a sentence.

I may get admission in a university.

He might eat an apple.

Passive voice

Admission may be got by me in a university.

An apple might be eaten by him.

NEGATIVE SENTENCES

I may not get admission in a university.

He might not eat an apple.

PASSIVE VOICE

Admission may not be got by me in a university.

An apple might not be eaten by him.

INTERROGATIVE SENTENCES

May I get admission in a university?

Might he eat an apple?

May admission be got by me in a university?

May an apple be eaten by him?

NEGATIVE AND INTERROGATIVE SENTENCE

May I not get admission in a university?

Might he not eat an apple?

May admission not be got by me in a university?

May an apple not be eaten by him?

Usage with must

I must get an admission in a university.

He must eat an apple.

An admission must be got by me in a university.

An apple must be eaten by him.

PRESENT CONTINUOUS DUBIOUS TENSE

A verb showing a dubitative condition of some continuous action in present time is called present continuous dubious tense.

Helping verbs:

May be, might be

Example:

Subject+maybe/might be+present participle verb+object.

He may be calling her.

John may be obscuring the secrets.

NEGATIVE SENTENCES

He may not be calling her.

John may not be obscuring the secrets.

INTERROGATIVE SENTENCES

May he be calling her?

May John be obscuring the secrets?

NEGATIVE AND INTERROGATIVE SENTENCE

May he not be calling her?

May John not be obscuring the secrets?

Usage with must

He must be calling her.

John must be obscuring the secrets.

PRESENT PERFECT DUBIOUS TENSE

A verb showing a dubitative condition of some action having completion in present or past time is called present perfect dubious tense.

Example:

Subject+may have/might have+past participle verb+object.

He may have called her.

John may have obscured the secrets.

Passive voice

She may have been called by him.

The secrets may have been obscured by John.

NEGATIVE SENTENCES

He may not have called her.

John may not have obscured the secrets.

PASSIVE VOICE

She may not have been called by him.

The secrets may not have been obscured by John.

INTERROGATIVE SENTENCES

May he have called her?

May John have obscured the secrets?

May she have been called by him?

May the secrets have been obscured by John?

NEGATIVE AND INTERROGATIVE SENTENCE

May he not have called her?

May John not have obscured the secrets?

May she not have been called by him?

May the secrets not have been obscured by John?

Usage with must

He must have called her.

John must have obscured the secrets.

She must have been called by him.

The secrets must have been obscured by John.

PRESENT PERFECT CONTINUOUS DUBIOUS TENSE

A verb showing a dubitative condition of some action which started in past and still continuing is called present perfect continuous dubious tense.

Example:

Subject+may have been/might have been+present participle verb+object.

He may have been calling her.

John may have been obscuring the secrets.

NEGATIVE SENTENCES

He may not have been calling her.

John may not have been obscuring the secrets.

INTERROGATIVE SENTENCES

May he have been calling her?

May John have been obscuring the secret?

NEGATIVE AND INTERROGATIVE SENTENCE

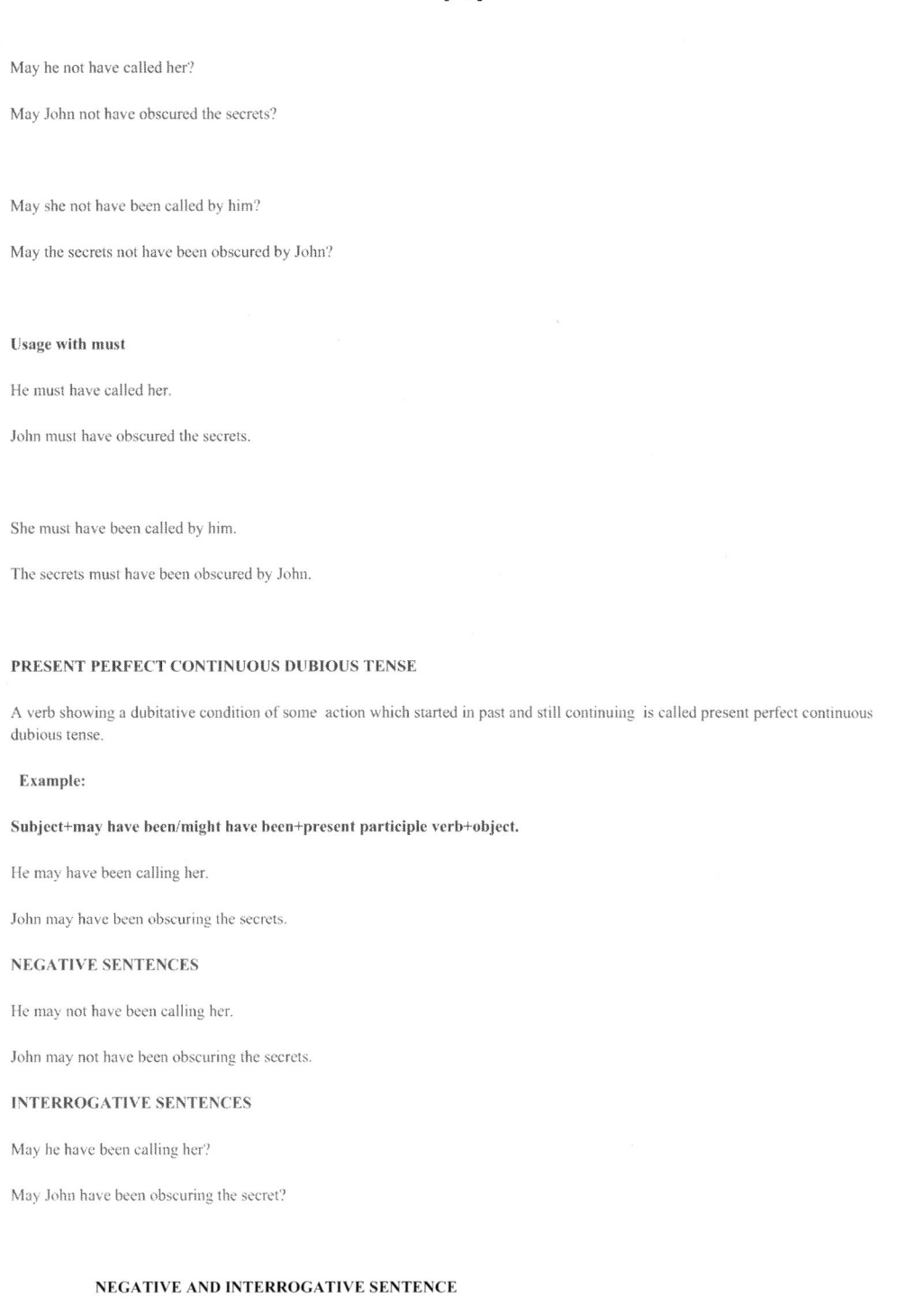

May he not have been calling her?

May John not have been obscuring the secret?

Usage with must.

He must have been calling her.

John must have been obscuring the secrets.

More usages of "May".

1. Permission

2. Pray

Example

1. May I come in?

2. May Allah give you good health!

We use question mark in first sentence and exclamation mark in second sentence.

* We can also use **shall** in question to ask for permission.

Shall I open it?

Shall we go now?

Shall I ask him a question?

Usage of "Must" and "have to".

To emphasize we use **must** in the sentence.

He must read a newspaper.

They must try getting another chance.

Azzan must play cricket during raining.

She must strive to get 1st position in her exams.

Have to used to say that something is required or necessary.

I have to read a newspaper. **Present**

They had to go to US. **Past**

She has to work hard.

John will have to call them. **Future**

PRESENT POTENTIAL TENSE

This tense signifies the ability of subject doing some work in present is called present potential tense.

Helping verbs:

Can

Example:

Subject+can+1st form of verb+object.

I can buy a car.

He can call them.

Passive voice

A car can be bought by me.

They can be called by him.

NEGATIVE SENTENCES

I can not buy a car.

He can't call them.

PASSIVE VOICE

A car can not be bought by me.

They can not be called by him

INTERROGATIVE SENTENCES

Can I buy a car?

Can he call them?

Can a car be bought by me.

Can they be called by him.

NEGATIVE AND INTERROGATIVE SENTENCE

Can I not buy a car?

Can't he call them?

Can't a car be bought by me?

Can they not be called by him?

PAST POTENTIAL TENSE

This tense signifies the ability of subject doing some work in past is called past potential tense.

Helping verbs:

Could

Example:

Subject+could+1st form of verb+object.

I could beat them.

He could call them.

Passive voice

They could be beaten by me.

They could be called by him.

NEGATIVE SENTENCES

I could not beat them

He couldn't call them.

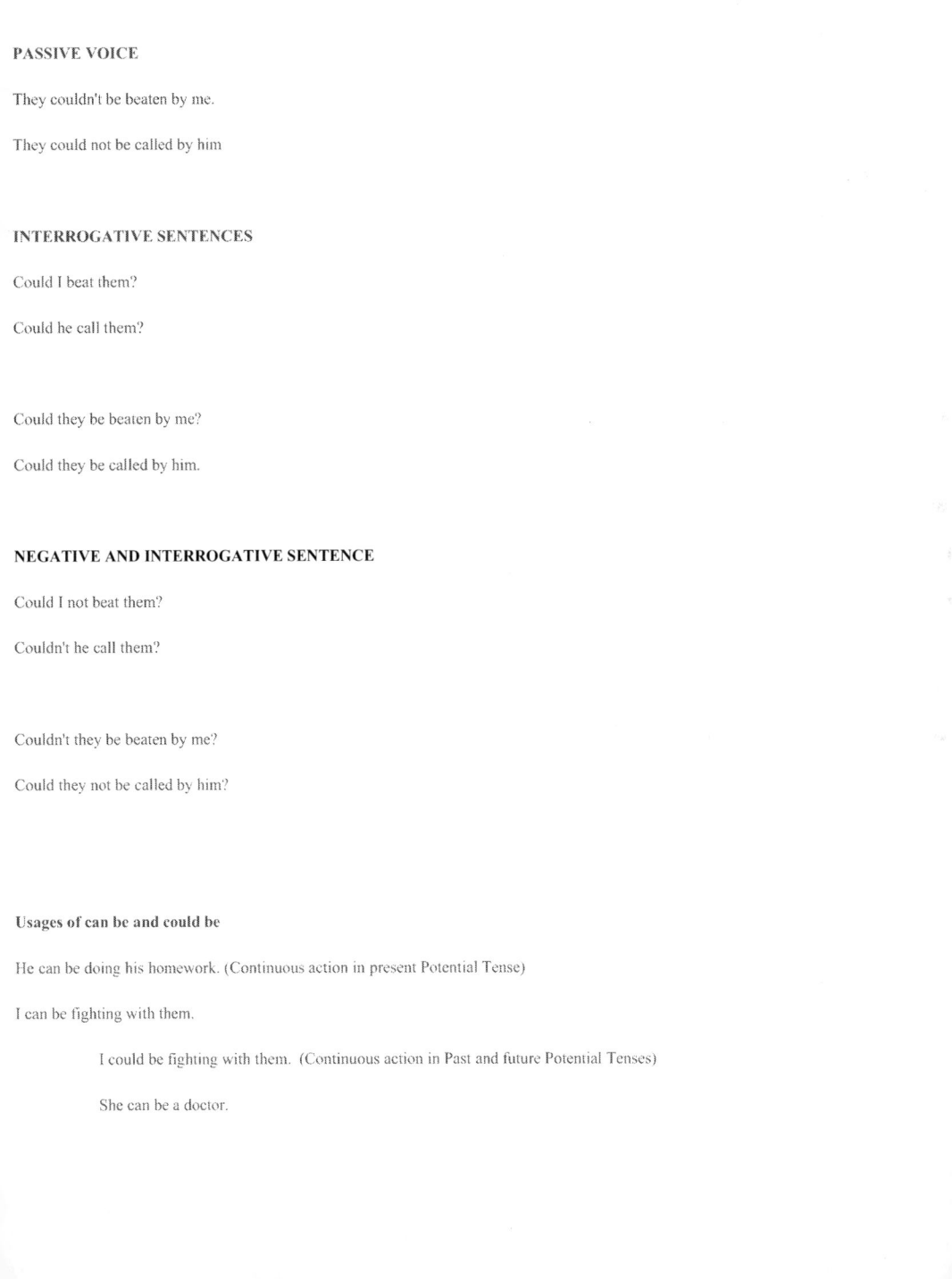

PASSIVE VOICE

They couldn't be beaten by me.

They could not be called by him

INTERROGATIVE SENTENCES

Could I beat them?

Could he call them?

Could they be beaten by me?

Could they be called by him.

NEGATIVE AND INTERROGATIVE SENTENCE

Could I not beat them?

Couldn't he call them?

Couldn't they be beaten by me?

Could they not be called by him?

Usages of can be and could be

He can be doing his homework. (Continuous action in present Potential Tense)

I can be fighting with them.

    I could be fighting with them. (Continuous action in Past and future Potential Tenses)

    She can be a doctor.

She could be a minister.

FUTURE POTENTIAL TENSE

This tense signifies the ability of subject doing some work in future is called future potential tense.

Helping verbs:

Could

Example:

Subject+could+1st form of verb+object.

Could or **could be** are also used for future.

He could call them.

I couldn't buy a car next year.

He could be doing his homework tomorrow.

Could I be fighting with them?

Could she not be a doctor one day?

He could become a minister in few years.

PASSIVE VOICE

He could call them.

I couldn't buy a car next year.

They could be called by him.

A car couldn't be bought by me next year.

Usages of couldn't have/ can't have

Couldn't have expresses past impossibility of an idea being true. It has a less complex range of meanings than can't have. **Can't have** tends to be used more in present contexts or contexts about recent situations or events, while **couldn't have** is used more in definitely past contexts.

Example:

They can't have broken the code.

I can't have bought a palace yet.

PASSIVE VOICE

The code can't have been broken by them.

A palace can't have been bought by me yet.

We couldn't have damaged her five years ago.

John couldn't have made money in business.

PASSIVE VOICE

She couldn't have been damaged by us five years ago.

Money couldn't have been made by John in business.

Usage Of should, should be, should have to, ought.

It shows the obligation.

I should talk to her.

Or

I should be talking to her.

We use "**ought**" with infinitive to show emphasis and obligation in the sentences.

America ought to mediate and resolve Kashmir issue.

He ought to take IELTS test in order to study abroad.

He should be a doctor.

They should be at home.

Or

They may be at home.

We use "**should have to**" to show necessity and obligation.

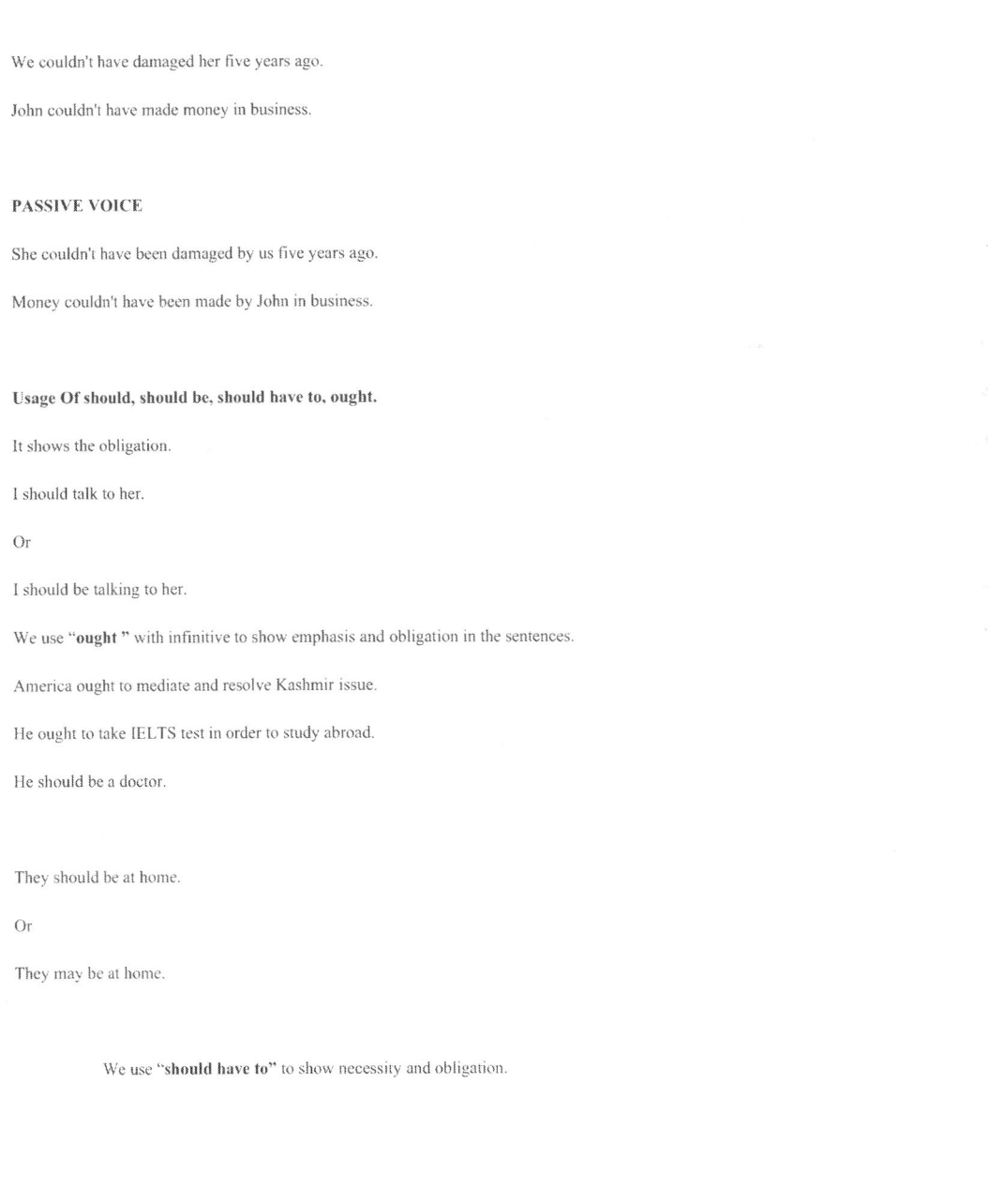

You should have to abide by rules.

He should have to apologize from her.

More usages of Should

Should you are selected, you will be informed soon. (Here Should means suppose)

Should you go to Karachi, what will you bring for me?

If you should meet him, don't tell him about me.

(Here Should means accidently by chance)

PRESENT HABITUAL TENSE

It shows habitual action in present time, also known as present tense.

Example:

Subject+1st form of verb+object.

He recites the Quran.

They read a newspaper.

Azzan likes to play cricket.

She always speaks truth.

PAST HABITUAL TENSE

It shows habitual action in past time is called past habitual tense.

Example:

1. Subject+used to+1st form of verb+object.

2. Subject+would+1st form of verb+object.

3. Subject+2nd form of verb+object.

1. I used to take tea.

Or

2. I would take tea.

Or

3. I took tea.

NEGATIVE SENTENCES

1. I used not to take tea.

Or

I didn't use to take tea.

2. I would not take tea.

3. I didn't take tea.

More uses of used to

I am used to taking tea.

Or

I am habitual of taking tea.

I am used to tea.

Or

I am habitual of tea.

Usage of Need/Dare

Need is used as a principal verb and as helping verb.

Need as a principal verb

It means require and it follows infinitive with to.

We need to call her.

I need to talk to him.

Need as auxiliary/helping verb

It remains unchanged whatever be the person or number of the subjects. It is common in question and negative sentences.

You need not ask my permission.

You needn't wait any longer.

Dare is used as a principal verb and as an auxiliary verb.

Dare as a principal verb

It is used in the sense of defy, challenge or face boldly and it is followed by infinitive with to.

She dared to swim across the river.

How does he dare to do it.

He dares to call her.

Dare as an auxiliary verb

It is followed by an infinitive without to. It is common in question and negative sentences.

He dare not do so. (**NOT he dares not do so.**)

He dare not take such a risk.

How dare he do such a thing.

CONDITIONAL SENTENCES

Normally conditional sentences are called conditionals. These sentences usually contain the conjunction IF. Sometimes they are called 'if clauses'.

There are mainly two types of conditionals.

Real and **unreal** conditionals

(Present Conditional Tense)

THE REAL CONDITIONALS

The real conditionals express factual or habitual conditions which have the possibility to occur in the future or generally occur in the present.

Example: (If clause is in present, second sentence is in future.).

* Meanings of both clauses will be in future.

If he gives me permission, I will buy a new car.

If they invite him, he will bring awesome gift for Alice.

I will fight with her, if she ignores me in the party.

If you do well in the exams, I will buy you a gift.

More uses of conditional sentences.

If he gives me permission, I can buy a new car.

If you do well in the exams, I may buy you a new car.

If he is coming home, I will accompany him.

If you invited me, I would attend a party along with my cousin. (S+Past tense+S+would+V+O)

If he bought a car, we would try food at the restaurants.

THE UNREAL CONDITIONALS

The unreal conditionals express hypothetical conditions which have no possibility to occur in the past, present or future but describe what could/might have occurred supposedly.

Example:

    If I were rich, I would travel my whole life.

    Or

    If I were rich, I were to travel my life.

* We can also use **were to** instead of **would** sentence in second clause.

If I had a car, I could go anywhere.

If I had the money, I would buy a new phone.

If I were the president, I would not support war policies.

PAST CONDITIONAL SENTENCES

Example:

Usage of would have, could have,

Should have, must have.

If+subject+had+past participle verb+object,

subject+would have/could have/should have/must have+past participle verb+object.

If he had taken loan from bank, he would have bought a new house.

If he had taken loan from bank, he could have bought a new house.

If I had called her, I should have talked to her.

If Alice had talked to me, she must have apologized for mistrust.

TRANSITIVE SENTENCES

Transitive verb takes a direct object; that is, the verb transmits action to an object.

He wrote a letter. (letter is direct object).
She promised me.(me is direct object).

INTRANSITIVE SENTENCES

An intransitive verb does not take an object.

He runs.
He complains frequently.
She sleeps.

* There is no object in above sentences. We don't do passive voice of intransitive sentences.

* One way to do passive voice is given below:
(Action of running is done by him).

GERUND

Gerund+verb+object.

Smoking is bad habit.
Killing is prohibited.
Writing makes me perfect.

INFINITIVE

Subject(infinitive)+verb

To smoke is prohibited.
To write makes me perfect.
To devise a strategy, will help succeed.

BARE INFINITIVE

Let, make, see, help, hear.

Let me call you tomorrow.
I will make you laugh at them
I will help you learn english language.
It will help succeed in a life.
I saw her fight with him.
I heard him talk against me.

STRUCTURES

CONJUNCTIVE SENTENCES

It shows that right after completing one task, started another task.

Example:

1. Having+past participle+object,+ subject+verb.

2. After having+past participle+object,+subject+verb.

Having read a newspaper, I had breakfast.

Or

After having read a newspaper, I had breakfast.

Or

After reading a newspaper, I had breakfast.

Having taken tea, I watched news on Tv.

Or

After having taken tea, I watched news on Tv.

Or

After taking tea, I watched news on Tv.

Having talked to her on phone, I wanted to meet her.

Or

After having talked to her on phone, I wanted to meet her.

Or

After talking to her on phone, I wanted to meet her.

PASSIVE VOICE

Having been appreciated, I started writing a book.

Having been blamed, Alice left the city.

* it means after getting appreciated, I started writing a book.

SENTENCES SHOWING COMMAND AND PLAN

Example:

Subject+to be+infinitive.

You are to finish homework within an hour.

(Command).

They are to reach Larkana by tomorrow.

(Plan)

He was to take IELTS test last month.

Exams are to commence from next month.

More Usage: Was to/ Were to, Was to have/Were to have.

He was to call her yesterday.

(He was going to call her yesterday but there is no confirmation, he called her or not).

He was to have called her yesterday.

(Its confirmed that he didn't call her yesterday)

OPTATIVE SENTENCES

It shows wish or desire in the sentences.

Example

1. Would that+subject+ were+complement.(Noun, Adjective)

2. If+subject+were+ complement.(Noun, Adjective)

We use **were** with all pronoun subjects.

1. Would that I were in New York.

Or

2. If I were in New York.

Would that he were president.

Or

If he were president.

EXCLAMATORY SENTENCES

It shows surprise, joy, grief, blessing or curse in the sentences.

Example:

What/how+noun/adjective+subject+verb.

What a cold! (Means there is very much cold)

How sweet she is! (She is very much sweet).

May Allah bestow you with children!

Hurray! I got 1st position in my exams!

Alas! He is dead!

CAUSATIVE SENTENCES

Causative is used when arranging for someone to do something for us.

Example

1. Indirect subject+get/have+object+past participle+by+direct subject.

I get my hair cut by hair cutter.

I have my hair cut by hair cutter.

2. Indirect subject+get/have+ direct subject+Infinitive/bare infinitive+object.

I get hair cutter to cut my hair.

I have hair cutter cut my hair.

NOT ONLY...BUT ALSO

To show more than one things, we use not only but also.

I am not only IT professional but also a writer.

He is not only young but also energetic.

They are not only old but also sick.

* Likewise We show some action in these sentences.

I not only read the articles but also write the articles.

He likes to not only drive a car but also ride on bycle.

EITHER/OR

To choose between two options or things, we use either/or.

I will bring either mobile phone or laptop for him.

Either he will call me or he will come to meet me.

EITHER

It describes any one of two things.

I will bring a book and newspaper, either of them will belong to you.

NEITHER/NOR

To show negativity between two actions or things.

I will bring neither of mobile phone nor laptop for him.(I will bring nothing for him).

Neither he will call me nor he will come to meet me.(he will not call me or he will not come to meet me).

NEITHER

To choose nothing between two things.

I will bring a book and newspaper, neither of them will belong to you.(nothing will belong to you).

NONE

There are many cars in the showroom, but none of them has navigation feature.(more than two choices , we use "**none**". Not even one of them)

BUT

"But" means "except" or "without" in the sentences.

I will go to US but you.

Or

I will go to US except/without you.

To show some action in the sentence after but.

We could not succeed but unite together.

Or

We could not succeed except unite together.

Or

We could not succeed without uniting together.

SCARCELY...WHEN

It shows that one action was going to complete meanwhile another action started.

Example:

Subject+scarcely+2nd form of verb, when+subject+2nd form of verb.

I scarcely wrote an article, when coronavirus started dispersing.

I scarcely graduated from a university when I got a job.

HARDLY/HARDLY EVER

Hardly means (degree) Barely, only just, almost not.

They hardly ever watch television.

I hardly ever go abroad.

I hardly think they'll come in this bad weather;

It's hardly possible he could lose the election.

LIKELY, SEEM , IT IS REPORTED , UNLIKELY.

1. You are likely to fly US in your life.

2. You seem to fly US in your life.

3. It is reported that US got affected with coronavirus more than any other country in the world in starting.

More usages

You are likely to have called her.

(Present perfect)

She is likely to have been called by you.

(Passive voice)

You're likely to be calling her.

(Present Continuous)

You are likely to call her.(Present)

She is likely to be called by you.(Passive voice)

Or

She is likely to get called by you.(Passive voice)

You are not likely to have called her.

Or

You are unlikely to have called her.

Or

You are likely to have not called her.

It seems unlikely that UK will accomplish brexit deal.

You're like to have been opposing them for long time.

He is likely to have been following you since you met him.

LIKE/UNLIKE

Like Pakistan, Afghanistan is also stabilizing its economy.

Like US, racial supremacist murder the Muslims in England.

Unlike Pakistan, India has won the world cricket cup often times.

Usage of Feel like

I feel like having tea. (I need to have tea now.)

I feel like taking a bite of it.

We feel like having dinner right now.

I feel like sleeping.

GONNA/GONNA GO/ WANNA

We can only use "gonna" when it is "helping" another verb to talk about an action in the future.

In the examples I just mentioned, the main verbs are **take**, and **buy**, and "gonna" (going to) is showing that these actions will happen in the future.

We're gonna take a walk,

She's gonna buy a car,

However, we CAN'T use "gonna" when "going to" is the MAIN VERB in the sentence.

For example, don't say:

I'm gonna New York tomorrow.

We're gonna a coffee shop after class.

They're gonna skiing on Saturday.

Using "gonna" as a helper for the main verb "go":

I'm gonna go to New York tomorrow.

We're gonna go to a coffee shop after class.

They're gonna go skiing on Saturday.

I wanna read a newspaper.

Or

I want to read a newspaper

Its gonna be delicious

Movie is gonna be interesting.

I Wanna be a doctor.

CAUSE

Students make many mistakes causing teacher to punish them.

Students who make many mistakes will cause the students to get punished by their teacher.

Or

Students who make many mistakes will cause the students to be punished by their teacher.

Usage of causing.

Causing+complement(noun/adjective)

There is wild fire in the forest causing huge loss in the city.

HAVING SAID THAT/ HOWEVER/ ON THE CONTRARY/ ON THE OTHER HAND

What is said in the first sentence, there should be a contradiction or contrast in the second sentence.

Alice backbites against John, having said that she is a good doctor.

Or

Alice backbites against John, however

 She is a good doctor.

Or

Alice backbites against John, on the contrary she is a good doctor.

SUBJUNCTIVE SENTENCES

Subjunctive is a special verb form that expresses something desired or imagined.

Example:

It Is suggested that Ali be sent abroad for specialization.

It is recommended that students be given the lectures online punctually.

Doctors be hired for coronavirus.

Police be depoliticized sooner.

If I were in the program, I would sing the song.

If I had billion of dollars, I would buy a big house.

I suggest that Alice write the article.

I propose that you be present at the meeting.

LEST...SHOULD

It shows that do one action otherwise there will occur another action. It shows kind of precaution and fear in the sentences.

Walk carefully lest you should fall down.

Work hard now lest you should fail in the exams later.

Get proper cure lest you should die.

Follow the corona precautions lest you should get affected with coronavirus.

IT IS TIME

To show the time of doing some thing.

It is time to leave.

It is time to sleep.

It is time to go to the hospital.

It is time to avail an opportunity.

* When it delays in doing something. We use following sentences.

It is time you married in your life.

(Means it is time you would have married in your life)

It is time we left for a university.

(Means it is time we would have left for a university)

It is time he took IELTS test.

(Means it is time he would have taken IELTS test.

AS THOUGH/AS IF

It shows unrealistic things in the sentence.

He walks as though he were president.

(He is not president)

He scares me as if he were criminal.

(He is not criminal)

They fight with him as though they were his enemies.

She acts as if she were an actor.

More usage of as if

He talked to her nicely as if he will propose her.

You are getting scared as if he will kill me.

Uses of Though.

Though he is innocent, they should give him another chance.

Though we are aware of racism, we will protest against the racists.

Though Pakistan is a developing country, US must collaborate with Pakistan in bussines.

EVEN THOUGH/ EVEN IF

He will not talk to her even though she calls him.

In above sentence, it shows that despite she calls him, he will not talk to her.

I will take care you even if I am out of city.

She will help you even though she is not rich.

WHETHER/OR

It shows two possibilities in the sentences.

You must take tea whether you feel like having tea or not.

She should talk to him whether she likes it or not.

IN CASE

I will call him in case there is something wrong.

I will help her in case she asks me.

He would have passed the exams in case he had strived.

UNTIL, UNLESS/UNTIL AND UNLESS.

Until means till (Up to the point in time).

They will accomplish their task until 1st October.

The result of the exams will be announced until Monday.

You can achieve the goal until you try.

She will prove herself until she is given a chance.

You will not succeed until you don't work hard.

Or

You will not succeed unless you work hard.

Or

You will not succeed until and unless you work hard.

* When we make negative sentence with "**until**" we use "helping verb" and "not".

* When we make negative sentence with "**unless**" we don't use "helping verb" and "not". We make affirmative sentence with "**unless**". But the sentence has a negative meaning. "**Until and unless**" is same as "**unless**".

SINCE/FOR

SINCE

It shows the point of time in the sentences.

I am tired since morning.

I am intellectual since my childhood.

I have tried to call her since yesterday.

I have been in Larkana since 2007.

FOR

It shows the period of time.

Police has been investigating him for a year.

I have been writing the articles for five years.

He has deceived her for two years.

I am here for an hour.

* To use **since** instead of **for**, we use **since** and put **ago** after time in the sentence.

* To use **for** instead of **since**, we use **for** and put **ago** after time in the sentence.

I have been in Larkana since 2007.

Or

I have been in Larkana for 2007 ago.

Police has been investigating him for a year.

Or

Police has been investigating him since a year ago.

AS SOON AS

As soon as+subject+verb subject+verb.

As soon as I saw your miscall I called you.

As soon as the guests came home, we served them a tea.

As soon as I woke up, I had a tea.

AS LONG AS

To show particular time in the sentences.

As long as you hate her, I will continue fighting with you.

As long as they don't get education, they will not be successful.

As long as I am here, I will keep supporting them.

TOO

She is too liar to be trusted.

Or

She is so liar that she can not be trusted.

He is too busy to call back.

Or

He is so busy that he can not call back.

You are too fatty to walk.

Or

You are so fatty that you can not walk.

AS FAR AS

To point out to particular thing or purpose in the sentences.

As far as I know the black hole in space connects this universe with other universes.

As far as I am concerned I will permit you.

As far as her friend I like her.

IF ONLY

It describes to talk about a wish to change something that has already occurred. It shows wish and hope in present and future.

If only she attends a party. (wish)

If only he accepts our invitation. (hope)

If only they speak a truth. (hope)

* It shows regret in past sentences.

If only he didn't blame them.

If only they spoke a truth.

If only we consulted with him.

PAST PERFECT

If only he had listened to what his friends had been telling him. (He didn't listen.)

If only Anna had been able to come. (Anna wasn't able to come.)

If only there was something she could do or say to help.

*We sometimes use were instead of was in more formal situations:

If only she weren't so tired. (If only she wasn't so tired.)

If only she were not my enemy .(If only she was not my enemy)

If only it were Saturday.(If only it was Saturday)

WAY+ADJECTIVE, WAY FORWARD,

WAY MORE/MUCH MORE/FAR MORE,

WAY TOO/MUCH TOO/FAR TOO

Way means "very".

He is way intelligent

Or

He is very intelligent.

They are way repellent.

Or

They are very repellent.

* **Way forward** means "leading to succeed".

His strategy is the way forward.

My idea was the way forward.

Way more/much more/ far more used with a comparison.

In **way more**, way means much or far.

He is way more/much more/ far more intelligent than her.

You have got way more talent.

He is way better/much better/far better than me.

You are way smarter.

Way too/much too/ far too.

In Way too, way means much or far and way adds to too meaning. It is used with Adjective.

This car is too expensive.

This car is way too expensive.(way adds to too)

The movie is much too short.

It is far too easy.

AS MUCH AS

My teacher told me to read as much as could.

I like her as much as she is my friend.

They are telling a lie as much as they can.

INSTEAD

I will make friends instead of enemies.

Instead of dinning out we ordered couple of pizzas.

I will call her instead of messaging her.

Instead, I asked a question.

Instead, she heard nothing from them.

ABOUT TO

I am about to fall down.(I am going to fall down)

We are about to take off.(We are going to take off)

We are about to leave the city.

They were about to kill him.

DIRECT SPEECH AND INDIRECT SPEECH

Direct speech is known as repeating the exact words spoken and Indirect speech is known as reporting the words.

Will, Shall, Can will change into Would, Should, Could. Present tense into Past tense, Past tense into Past tense, will into would.

He said to me, "I will call her".(Direct speech)

He said that he would call her. (Indirect speech)

She said," I will take IELTS test". (Direct speech)

She said that she would take IELTS test.(Indirect speech)

They said," we give her response. (Indirect speech)

They said that they gave her response. (Direct speech)

HELP

It shows that one can not desist from doing something.

He can't help smoking.

I can't help praising your beauty.

They couldn't help backbiting against him.

I can't help it.

NEVERTHELESS/ NONTHELESS/ NOTWITHSTANDING

These words mean in spite of or despite.

They opposed me, nevertheless I will talk to them.

He fought with me, nonetheless I will talk to him.

Alice backbit against us, notwithstanding we will rely on her.

Usage of "Having to+Verb"

"Have to" is a modal verb which is used to indicate something which happens regularly whereas "having to" is a continuous action happening for a shorter period of time due to a need or requirement.

Pakistan is having to reform all its institutions.

Or

Pakistan has to reform all its institutions.

We are having to ask him few questions.

Or

We have to ask him few questions.

Alice is having to pretend to be their friend.

Or

Alice has to pretend to be their friend.

John is having to give an interview for job.

Or

John has to give an interview for job.

Usage of Were, Were to.

This shows wish and possibility in unreal past.

If I were leader, I would develop Pakistani economy.

I he were rich, he would buy you a new house.

If I were to lead the party, I would make the party succeed.

I they were to kill her, Police would detain them.

Made in the USA
Columbia, SC
07 May 2023

ad9a4cd8-4552-43a2-b798-ae908663751fR02